PRIEST TURNED THERAPIST TREATS FEAR OF GOD

Also by Tony Hoagland

POETRY

Recent Changes in the Vernacular
Application for Release from the Dream
Unincorporated Persons in the Late Honda Dynasty
What Narcissism Means to Me
Donkey Gospel
Sweet Ruin

ESSAYS

Twenty Poems That Could Save America and Other Essays
Real Sofistikashun: Essays on Poetry and Craft

PRIEST TURNED THERAPIST TREATS FEAR OF GOD

Tony
Hoagland

POEMS

Graywolf Press

This publication is made possible, in part, by the voters of Minnesota through a Minnesota State Arts Board Operating Support grant, thanks to a legislative appropriation from the arts and cultural heritage fund, and a grant from the Wells Fargo Foundation. Significant support has also been provided by Target, the McKnight Foundation, the Lannan Foundation, the Amazon Literary Partnership, and other generous contributions from foundations, corporations, and individuals. To these organizations and individuals we offer our heartfelt thanks.

Published by Graywolf Press
250 Third Avenue North, Suite 600
Minneapolis, Minnesota 55401

www.graywolfpress.org

Published in the United States of America

ISBN 978-1-55597-807-5

2 4 6 8 9 7 5 3 1
First Graywolf Printing, 2018

Library of Congress Control Number: 2017953461

Cover design: Kyle G. Hunter

Cover art: Pahari School Painting of Dipak Raga

For Kathleen Lee

CONTENTS

I.

II.

III.

IV.

PRIEST TURNED THERAPIST TREATS FEAR OF GOD

What does a worker lack? Weil once asked this question, and then answered: "The science of his affliction."

FANNY HOWE

Come again shining glance in your good time

W. S. MERWIN

I.

ENTANGLE

Sometimes I prefer not to untangle it.
I prefer it to remain disorganized,

because it is richer that way
like a certain shrubbery I pass each day on Reba Street

in an unimpressive yard, in front of a house that seems unoccupied:
a chest-high, spreading shrub with large white waxy blossoms—

whose stalks are climbed and woven through simultaneously
by a different kind of vine with small magenta flowers

that appear and disappear inside the maze of leaves
like tiny purple stitches.

The white and purple combination of these species,
one seeming to possibly be strangling the other,

one possibly lifting the other up—it would take both
a botanist and a psychologist to figure it all out,

—but I prefer not to disentangle it,
because it is more accurate.

My ferocious love, and how it repeatedly is trapped
inside my fear of being sentimental;

my need to control even the kindness of the world,
rejecting gifts for which I am not prepared;

my apparently inextinguishable notion
that I am moving toward a destination

—I could probably untangle it
yet I prefer to walk down Reba Street instead

in the sunlight and the wind, with no mastery
of my feelings or my thoughts,

purple and ivory and green, not understanding what I am
and yet in certain moments remembering, and bursting into tears,

somewhat confused as the vines run through me
and flower unexpectedly.

A WALK AROUND THE PROPERTY

There are too many characters in this book I'm reading.
I can't keep track of them all.
How can I care who marries who, or what they wear?
Nevertheless, each time one disappears, I feel a brief, sharp grief,
knowing they will not return.

This is how a boat drifts out to sea from shore.
It gets distracted and detached, pulled this way and that by currents.
Eventually, not even pain can guide it home.

I will tell you this right now: Cincinnati
has not been a great success for me.
My allergic reaction to small talk has ensured
that I don't get asked to parties anymore.
My deep curiosity about other people has gone unslaked.

How did Ellen, who hates to be touched, get pregnant?
Who is Sam in love with? Is Emily gay?
What does my neighbor do at 3 a.m., when his office light is on?
Was I wrong to think of life as work?

"Sing me a song about the world!"
says the therapist, as he looks out at the thunder and the rain,
a little glum about his only half-effective science.
He has no cured clients.

The moon shines down from the black November sky.
The tide rises like a sweeping, white-ruffed arm,
erasing all the pages that have come before.
The evidence accumulates that nobody is watching over us,

and gradually, as the streets and houses drift toward night,
all the words inside them close their eyes;
the sentences coil up like snakes and sleep.

It's just me now and my famous aching heart
under the stars—my heart that keeps moving like a searchlight
in its longing for the hearts of other people,
who in a sense, already live there, in my heart,

and keep it turning.

THE ROMANCE OF THE TREE

It wasn't the dream of the enormous spruce tree
to be turned into fifty reams of paper
then stacked and cut and bound into 4" X 6" format pages,

and printed with the sentences
of a seething hot romance novel
called *Summertime Nurses*.

Season after season, while the tree was growing tall,
while it breathed and swayed among its brethren other trees,
it wasn't dreaming of becoming the delivery device

for a steamy bedroom episode
in which the small deft hands of someone named Brittany
"unbuttoned her jeans with feverish impatience."

Oh tree, you were part of the forest for years,
bending and straightening and bending
like the mast of a great ship—
tasting the earth with your long dark roots.

That was a different story indeed
from the one printed on page 38
in which the exchange student from Norway

enters the dark lounge of the Carterville Inn,
and just stands there like Apollo by the Budweiser sign
inflaming the entire female populace of Tweedy County.

When the tree was cut down and hauled away to the mill
to be turned into *Summertime Nurses*,
we lost part of our Eden

worth more than a paperback;
the tree, swaying all day in the sun,
rocked and pushed by the wind,

yielding and tousled under the white clouds,
with all of its arms outstretched,
all of its mouths wide open.

HAPPY AND FREE

I should not have gotten the tattoo that says
May All Beings Be Happy and Free on my left arm,
running from the inside of my elbow to the wrist
in 20 pt. Verdana sans-serif type.

My serotonin level that day was so elevated
that it deceived me
into an optimistic feeling that I was finally
ready to be pure. I have been happy in that way before

and you would think I would have learned by now
that I inevitably return to earth
like a leaky, gradually deflating helium balloon.

Now I see that my great tattoo might better have been
a customized sweatshirt purchased online for twenty dollars,
that said *Short Attention Span,*
or *University of Repetitive Emotion.*

How quickly things pass. How long mistakes last.
How unrealistic I am when left to my own devices.
When I rolled up my shirt sleeve at the tattoo emporium
to have that sentence stenciled into my pale flesh

I was getting into a relationship
I could not possibly sustain.
May All Beings Be Happy and Free—what a fitting punishment
for the hubris of my passing and unstable self-esteem!

And yet, it is my life, mine to squander as I will.
—That is a kind of freedom, I suppose.
And I have a story, which is still
unfinished;

that makes me kind of happy, too.

WHICH WOULD YOU PREFER,
A STORY OR AN EXPLANATION?

I am interested, said Madeline, in people's ability to live their lives
                                        in fragments.

Two ex-husbands, three jobs in seven years, one daughter,
                        a geranium, and a certain TV show.

I used to think I'd reach a certain age, said Madeline,
and my heart would settle down, like a tired dog.

Yoga at the Y on Tuesdays;
then wild gusts of anger while driving home.

Reading an interview with Allan Bloom, she learns
that "the pursuit of happiness is a particularly American form of
                                        nihilism."

"Oh yeah, now you tell me," she says.

"I can't tell the difference between inner peace and mild depression,"
writes her friend from Philadelphia, in small blue script
on the back of a postcard of Chagall.

Dawn arrives on the horizon with its spreading rosy light.
Sometimes beauty serves as a kind of anesthetic.
The world provides evidence for almost anything.
Which would you prefer: a story or an explanation?

In the next two years, Madeline will have a love affair,
visit Bali and return, develop endometrial cancer,

and reconnect with her childhood Catholic faith,
worth more to her than anything.

Even at the bottom of the self, even in illness and despair;
in hubris, ecstasy and gloom,

the chick can be heard inside the shell,
pecking to get out. Pecking and pecking.

NOBILITY

In the 3,000 letters written by Virginia Woolf between 1930 and 1941,
she does not once express anxiety about the size of her rear end.

"To have aesthetics," says Robert, "is to be a snob.
To be above certain things—even parts of yourself."

Aldous Huxley on his deathbed, unable to speak,
writes on a white pad to Evelyn, his wife: the note:
                              "100 micrograms mescaline, IM."

She nods and brings it back in an hour—
I tell this story several times to Kath, until I am sure she gets my point.

Walking in Jackson Park, I find a great two-hundred-year-old oak,
extending its huge dark limbs in all directions, like an antler
                              or a chandelier.

I stand and stare at it, as at a letter in an alphabet I have forgotten.
But I am a creature who still has not learned to read
—not even to worship, not even to live without dishonesty.

The nurse's aide says, "Did we have a bowel movement today,
                              Mr. Mandela?"
and he looks at her with so much tolerance and calm,
it is like the sea looking back at the land.

In the cancer clinic waiting room, the patients are mostly quiet.
Sometimes they talk about the football game,
                              or the weather predicted for tomorrow.

NO THANK YOU

Wisdom isn't scarce; it
never was. The average bookshelf
of a Psych major named James
at Cumberland Community College
will yield all the wisdom

that was ever necessary
to end war, teach kindness,
face death,
sprout honesties

like flowers, fashion
codes of understanding for a
working world.
We have

everything we need,
don't know what the
hell it is, don't want it, won't
remind each other, refuse
to listen.

What makes it worse
are the constant bulletins
from all those liars who keep saying,
        We are looking

for solutions—Getting
close to—Poised
to make the
breakthrough—Any day now.
                Not true. We

already have chosen the strange
garments of confusion
that we will die in; we love
the thrill of enemies;
we burn

through beauty like it was
wrapping paper;
we breathe
the smoke of our distraction
like it was oxygen.

So this morning,
I will just
walk into the woods off Marsden Lane,
seize a clump of dirt and pine-straw
in my fist,
and kneel,

in a manner no different from
any peasant in a jerkin
in the fourteenth century
asking for salvation—

saying, *Preserve me, God,*
at least
from the pretense
that I am searching.

I am lost by choice
and
all the evidence suggests
I relish it.

PROOF OF LIFE

Those small cuts and infections on my hands from splinters and thorns
that show I have been working out of doors this week.

The maddening peculiar purgatory
of Bob Seger and the Silver Bullet Band playing "Against the Wind"

continuously for three days inside my head,
until on the fourth day it finally stops.

The sound of clothes going around in the dryer
at the other end of the house.

Wanting from a very young age
not to be a zombie sleepwalking through time.

Leaving people, and being left by them.
This catch-and-release version of life.

The kidnappers send out a photograph of the hostage, grimacing,
holding up a newspaper from yesterday.

They call this "proof of life."
It means the captive is still alive.

The day is blue with one high white cloud
like a pilgrim going to Canterbury.

There is a bird half-hidden in the shrub outside.
Something he has eaten has made his chest feathers red.

DISTANT REGARD

If I knew I would be dead by this time next year
I believe I would spend the months from now till then
writing thank-you notes to strangers and acquaintances,

telling them, "You really were a great travel agent."
Or "I never got the taste of your kisses out of my mouth."
Or "Watching you walk across the room was part of my destination."

It would be the equivalent, I think,
of leaving a chocolate wrapped in shiny foil
on the pillow of a guest in a nice hotel—

"Hotel of earth, where we resided for some years together,"
I start to say—before I realize it is a terrible cliché, and stop,
and then go on, forgiving myself in a mere split second

because now that I'm dying, I just go
forward like water, flowing around obstacles
and second thoughts, not getting snagged, just continuing

with my long list of thank-yous
which seems to naturally expand
to include sunlight and wind,

and the aspen trees which seethe and shimmer in the yard
as if grateful for being soaked last night
by the beautiful irrigation system

invented by an individual
to whom I am quietly grateful.
Outside it is autumn, the philosophical season,

when cold air sharpens the intellect;
the hills are red and copper in their shaggy majesty.
The clouds blow overhead, like governments and years.

It took me a long time to understand the phrase "distant regard,"
but I am grateful for it now,
and I am grateful for my heart,

that turned out to be good, after all;
and grateful for my mind,
to which, in retrospect, I can see

I have never been sufficiently kind.

PRIEST TURNED THERAPIST
TREATS FEAR OF GOD

For once the weatherman was right:
cold morning, cloudy afternoon;
tomorrow the city will be buried
under tons of fine white snow.

Why not just turn the radio off
and make up your own news?
"The President today in Washington
took off his shirt for reporters
to show his big muscles and hairy back."

He said the CEO of China has made him very mad;
he's going to beat the stuffing
out of that no-good Jap.

Then he said that little boy with cancer
rescued from the avalanche
is what makes this country so darn great.

In other news, Ignorance Industry scientists
have recorded a decrease in the quality of ignorance.
There are more ignorant people than ever,
but the totality of ignorance continues to decline.
What does it mean?

Here are our other leading stories:
Unidentified Rich Man Elected President;
San Francisco Yoga Tragedy: Three People Hugged to Death;
Priest Turned Therapist Treats Fear of God.

In Hollywood, fifty movie stars have pledged
not to use their swimming pools
until world thirst is ended.

To keep it short:
Diet   Celebrity   Money   Pregnancy   Explosion
It all seemed pretty much business as usual.
That's why we were happy to be indoors,
sipping our green mint tea;

sitting by the window,
and watching the sky fall down.

II.

IN THE WAITING ROOM WITH LEONARD COHEN

In the hospital waiting room, seated in my plastic chair,
I think about Leonard Cohen and start quietly to cry.
I'm glad no one is watching, because I can see

the childish indulgence of it all—the displacement of my personal self-pity
onto the cadaverous Canadian singer
whom one critic called "the world's leading producer
                              of songs advocating suicide."

Yet it comes from somewhere deep, this sobbing
sympathy for Leonard Cohen,
and I don't care if it's dishonest, there is nourishment

in these wet tears. I sense
I'm irrigating my own dirty life
with something clean and fresh, like rain, from far away.

Still, crying is violent and weird and hard.
It is like pulling something free from something else
that doesn't want to give it up,
and keeps on pulling back with a wheezing, ripping sound.

Outside the window,
it's not quite sleeting in the gray morning
and I see umbrellas popping open far below;

the sidewalks slowly growing dark and stained with wet,
as cabs speed through the gloom with headlights on.

I'm not doing that well in this waiting room today,
but I'm glad that Leonard Cohen is here,
because I feel like I'm stuck half inside and half out

of one of his songs—
a place where angels have not been seen in years;
where ugliness presents itself with a kind of roguish charm.

In the reflection of the window,
I see his face—his furrowed mouth, the wet black eyes
and that great curved hatchet of a nose:

an expert witness on the death of God;
a master at the art of being broken
in order to be made.

Who would have imagined?
Me in the hospital, with Leonard Cohen,
and still too ignorant to die;

still trying to learn a few of these fundamental things
before the pallbearers arrive:

What Grief Is Good For;
What Imagination Can and Cannot Do.
How to work with this suspicion
that I am the one responsible

for letting the dove out of the coffin.

TEN QUESTIONS FOR THE NEW AGE

Why does someone who takes the name Buffalo Vision, for example,
after his weekend ayahuasca workshop

always seem to have an unwarranted confidence
that he is going to end up at the Happy Hunting Ground?

If Seymour Eagle Mountain marries Western River Woman—fine.
But why do they have to name their daughter Blueberry, or Lake?

Then they send her to suffer at a Waldorf School
where she majors in birch bark and folk dance

and years later has to hire a life coach to help her fill out college
                                        applications,
as she painstakingly writes an autobiographical essay

on the theme of how certain so-called sentient beings
can inflict their embarrassing illusions upon another.

Do you get what I'm talking about?
About the hazards of playing at innocence?

Walt Disney made some good movies,
but would you really get five sayings from *The Lion King*

tattooed on your forearm for practical reference
as you ship out to Iraq?

Which brings me to my actual subject, a man I will call Connor,
whom I met at a rest stop right after his second vision quest;

who wore a feather in his hat, was fifty-five, well-fed,
and lived with his mom in Carson City; who

plays his guitar at open mikes and plans on a serious musical career
as soon as he gets more experience.

Connor, who prefers to be called by his true name, Iron Bear.
Whenever I encounter the New Age still in its original diapers,

I confess that I blush down to my deepest roots,
for I, too, am its scornful, not entirely grown-up child;

when I was twenty, I learned to play "Blowin' in the Wind" on a
                              wooden flute;
I made bracelets out of hemp and polished quartz, and gave them away;

I had a girlfriend who freely expressed her opinion
that people born in Bangladesh had probably incarnated there

to work out their issues with poverty.

Why does the New Age seem so often like a patient in intensive care,
in a delicate condition, requiring giant infusions

of illusion and charity to stay alive,

while the rest of us keep waiting for the day it might get tough enough
to be successfully transplanted into the real world?

Getting back to Connor, still living with his mom, on an allowance,
                              in Carson City:
nothing can stop him

from going to the open mike every Thursday night and singing his
                              heart out,
or from signing his letters *Blessings,* from *Iron Bear, Poet and Seer,*
                              aka Connor.

Pretend for a moment that you are a philanthropist whom I am
asking for a donation to a charitable program

to rehabilitate wandering middle-aged children like the ones I am
                              describing.
What funds can you offer? What advice might you have for me?

What chance do you think there is for Connor to ever grow up,
much less to find a happy ending?

On the other hand, isn't it some kind of ultimate foolishness
to scold cheerful people who in their way are the pilgrims of our time

about the folly of their happiness?
I ask you—what kind of folly is that?

TEN REASONS WHY WE CANNOT SEEM
TO MAKE PROGRESS

As long as the cheerleader keeps watching the movie about cheerleaders
and the businessman keeps a copy of *The Art of War* in his attaché case.

As long as the money retains no memory of where it has been
but keeps on running like a river.

Until going to war is explained in terms of child development.

Until the male character in the novel is shown licking his fingers
and reaching down to brush the woman's cunt until

her wetness wakes and matches his.

Until every candidate for Congress is required
to work for a year in the hospital,
                              rubbing lotion into the stumps of the amputees,

which is so frightening to the men on a sexual level
that soon only women will run for office.

As long as meaning is hunted and killed and
placed on display like a trophy head on the wall.

As long as shoppers enter the heaven of the shopping mall
like ants climbing in a long line

into the nozzle of the plastic honey container,
to die in a golden profusion
                              of what they planned to bring back with them.

As long as there are these things
we are not able to notice or think, or say out loud

—because until we can say them,
we will be trapped inside the dream.

EPISTLE OF MOMENTARY GENEROSITY

I get a note from James, who used to be my friend,
in which he says he misses me,

so I hold the letter in my hand,
and for a moment just appreciate

this kindness that he squeezed out of his heart
right before that muscle clenched again

and tried to make him take it back,
or add a note that says, *You dirty snake.*

You have my Leonard Cohen albums.

And thus are human beings:
not always frightened and unkind. We

have moments when the mind unclouds
and old injuries are forgiven;

when the policeman hands the criminal a cigarette
and they stand in place and smoke, and stare

out the window at the rain;
when the lifejacket is tossed

from the back deck of a ship
too big to turn around—good luck!

That freely given impulse—there it goes.
An hour later, you might regret your

open-handedness, or think it weak,
but it is gone; the blessing

can't be taken back,
and like a gull it sails

over the churning ocean,
tilting sideways for an instant

to slip between the judgment cliffs.

A SHORT HISTORY OF MODERN ART

The Green Owl Café—I think that is
where I first heard the name of Giacometti;
"Giacometti," reverently pronounced by some guy in a goatee and beret,

smoking a clove cigarette and holding forth
on the plight of modern man,
trying to convince some vampire girl stenciled with tattoos

to come back to his coffin with him.
"Do you feel me, baby?" he was purring into her ear,
"Nobody does real like Giacometti."

After that I went to the museum
and built a little more
Giacometti into my vocabulary,

Giacometti, who represented the idea of *human*
in the phrase *human condition*
as a kind of burn victim

standing on two legs like blackened crutches
in a landscape of barbed wire and concentration camps.
Somewhere in there I got the notion

that Giacometti's sculptures must be a strange self-portrait.
Somewhere in Italy I imagined an anorexic guy
with an acetylene torch

was wandering the countryside,
welding one spidery
skeleton after another

out of fire-blackened metal.
Then I heard a song called "Giacometti" on the radio,
in which the heavy, angst-saturated hook

was, *Every human being is trying to decide*
whether to become a cannibal or a suicide.

I was 17—my mother was dead; my head
was a smokestack full of rage and fear.
I understood that people were dishonest and confused;

the soul pitch-dark—the world unsafe.
The human prognosis was not that great.
That's when Giacometti

showed up to help me out.
The good news was that
someone had figured out

a way to take the bad news
and turn it into art.

THEATER PIECE

The good white people of the Triangle Theatre Company
have decided they need a black performance artist
for their autumn gala

so they advertise, and soon artists of color
line up outside the theatre door for the audition,
volunteering to be exploited for a reasonable sum,

doing hip-hop sonnets that rhyme *cotton* with *rotten*.
Waiting for his interview, the playwright from Georgia
knows there is something problematical

about trading his grandparents' story
for a place in the culture establishment,
but he listens attentively

as the board of directors explains to him
that their theatre wants to embrace diversity
but not be abrasive to their audience.

—They don't want one of those pieces
that makes historical injustice
into a big pile of crap dumped

in the middle of the stage.
Yes, the playwright understands their concerns.
He says he can give them the story

of a voodoo queen from Sierra Leone
who helped protect others on the Middle Passage.
Or he can give them a fairy tale

in the voices of rabbits and crows
who overcome prison and addiction,
but he won't give unlimited shoeshines

to white millionaires with season
tickets to the Coliseum.
Then they sit at the table looking at each other,

the buyers and sellers,
tangled in feelings and thoughts from the past.
They sit at the table in a dizzy silence

in which trust feels like a pair of shackles
they have volunteered to fasten
to their own ankles with a click

because they do not see any other way
to get into the future together.

COUTURE

If by mink

coat you mean

a soft, warm

garment

made from

the lives of

many other

creatures,

then, yeah, sure,

I guess you

could say I'm

wearing a

mink coat.

AN ORDINARY NIGHT IN ATHENS, OHIO

Those children in pajamas
in the big suburban houses

are not dreaming
of fireflies in jars,

nor model cars,
but of fist-fighting

on Mars
in bodies not their own;

they are not feeding the hamster
small bits of lettuce

and changing its name
from Joe to Josephine, and back,

but sprinting over the rooftops
of burning Dairy Queens

and aiming shoulder-launched rockets
into shopping malls.

They are not dreaming
of taking the quiz

and getting deeply hung up
on the answer to question four,

but of yellow school buses
wrapped in ruptures of flame,

and of playmates they knew
in second grade

floating facedown
over the dimes and tarnished pennies

in the wishing fountain.

INEXHAUSTIBLE RESOURCE

"After the ocean rises, all this will be underwater,"
the biologist was saying, spreading her hands in the café,

"—by which I mean," she clarified, "scuba diving in Manhattan:
floating past the stone gargoyles on the Chrysler Building,
swimming in and out the windows of Trump Tower."

No reason to get agitated, says the Buddhist at the table;
Even the expression "global warming" is a case
$\qquad\qquad\qquad\qquad\qquad$ *of planetary-centrism.*

. . .

Carnage of the elephants and whales
Pandemic of the insects and the frogs
Scourging of the coral reefs and glaciers
Pillage of the rivers and the lakes
Eradication of crickets in the swamp, and
The fog hanging in the arms of coastal cypresses

. . .

As John Keats, in his last letter, wrote,
"I have a feeling of my real life being past,
$\qquad\qquad$ and that I am already living my posthumous existence."

. . .

Even in these days before the coming storm,
our anguish, our handwringing and laments,
our statistical reports and scientific fights,

—can someone tell me, please
why they feel like a performance?

. . .

Imagination, our last system of immunity.
Disbelief, our most inexhaustible resource.
Unreality, my great love, protect me.

ACHILLES

Achilles is being carried from the field.
Three-fourths covered by a thin green gown; one
                                    big bare shoulder sticking out,
his face ash-gray and ivory-pale.
His war is finished. They're taking him home.

They have him in the bay across from me
on a gurney outside Radiology. IV bags suspended over his head
like toy Mylar balloons fastened to his arms by string.
Anyone can see he's done.

It seems we are temporarily encamped upon the bank
of that famous river that has run
through London and Detroit, Bangkok and Baghdad—
this Ganges down which a hundred million souls have gone
like candles flickering in mist.

Our brave companions here: the cornrowed orderly from Birmingham;
the plump Filipina nurse; Myron who spends his check on Powerball;
the weeping relatives. They move among us whispering.

Achilles—his name is called at last—
is being wheeled now on his way
into the crypt-cold vault called Radiology.

They roll him past. Maybe I am the only one
who sees the six tall ghosts that walk on either side of him,
rhythmically striking their fists against their shields.
I want to say, *Look, don't pity him! His imagination is not dead!*

Sideways, going by, he opens one of his gray eyes
to look at me, and raises two fingers in that salute
I am coming to recognize.

And then I am here alone,
the one to weep,
and it is myself I weep for.

EXAMPLES OF JUSTICE

Aspirin,
crack cocaine,
the poetry of Keats;
Kathleen's big beautiful face,
and *The Communist Manifesto*
—these are all pain relievers.

Death from cancer of the mouth
of the tyrant Joseph McCarthy;
the blue crow gliding over the arroyo, cawing;
the baby taking the lima bean from his mouth
and pushing it back between the lips of his mother
—these are examples of justice.

The moment when you step away from the party;
the sound of the eighty-foot spruce tree, creaking;
the hour in the waning afternoon
when the attorney stands beside her car,
removes her sunglasses, and looks up at the sky
—these are examples of remembering.

The metaphor that makes you laugh out loud.
The warm breast of the dental hygienist
pressed against your ear
as she leans to get access to your plaque.

The dream in which you find yourself at sea,
at night, with water under you so deep
you weep with fear. And yet the darkness
does not take you into it
—these are examples of fortune.

BETTER THAN EXPECTED

Things were not as bad as I had thought.
The scrape in the fender of the rented car
could be hidden with a little white paint
before I returned it to the agency.

This CD of New Age music, which I disliked at first,
with its synthetic wind of pulsing jellyfish,
does a remarkable job of slowing down my heart.

Merely to have survived to this point
is already the most unlikely triumph;
to still be breathing and trying to improve.

Things are definitely better than expected.
I'm not on trial for anything.
I have given up on the idea of great success.
The oncologist says the X-ray shows no "abnormalities."

We are always trying to come to a decision,
always in a place where we are making up our minds
whether the soup is good, the flowers pretty,
whether we are fortunate or poor.

All my life I have been
          loved by women,
                    held up by water,
                              ignored by war.
I have outlasted the voluntary numbness
I required in order to remain alive.

Why shouldn't I be able,
why shouldn't I be able *now*,
to walk down the street,

under the overhanging trees
and raise my arms and say
that the rain shaking down from the leaves

is not an inconvenience but a joy?

III.

THE TRUTH

In summer there was something in the selfhood of the wasps
that wanted to get inside the screened-in porch.
It sent them buzzing against the wire mesh,

probing under the eaves,
crawling into the cracks between the boards.
Each day we'd find new bodies on the sill:

little failures, like struck matches:
shrunken in death, the yellow
color of cider or old varnish.

The blue self of the sky looked down
on the self of the wooden house
where the wasps were perishing.
The wind swept them to the ground.

The wasps seemed to be extensions
                                of one big thing
making the same effort again and again.

I can remember that feeling of being driven
by some longing I could not understand
to look for the passage through,

—trying again and again
to get inside. I must have left a lot
of dead former selves scattered around behind me

while I kept pushing my blunt head
at a space that prevented my entering
—and by that preventing delivered me

to where I live now, still outside;
still flying around
in the land of the unfinished.

FROG SONG

I go out on the porch to smoke and listen
to the voices of dead fathers from the marsh beyond the trees.

They are reborn as bullfrogs, and at a certain hour of the night
they begin to speak with disproportionate satisfaction

from the warm porridge of the swamp, where they believe
that they are geniuses and kings,

having discovered an unexpected gift for throat-singing,
and an ability to love themselves they were denied in human life.

This humid, starry night; a zillion crickets shimmeringly shrill
like an enormous diagnosis of tinnitus.

Around each light, a swirl of moths; above the trees, the
spiraled galaxies

against which my own unhappiness
is such a bunch of small potatoes

as to be a form of humor.

Father—go take your place among your kind,
content in the oily moistness of your skin,

replete in your ability to catch the quickest bugs.
I would have loved you more, if only I had known

you were a frog—amphibious, mottled, and small-brained;
not intimate by nature; preferring

to stay half-immersed below the water line;
so much a part of nature's plan you are oblivious to it.

Tonight, under the varnished, punctured skein of sky,
where the moon is rising in a humid daze,

we crouch,
singing our midnight song.

SCOTCH TAPE

There's a radio station at the left end of the dial
where you can listen to 24 hours of genocide and war crimes;
how in the south the election was bought cheap

by men in unmarked uniforms;
how the contaminated medicine was shipped abroad,
until babies started being born with deformed spines.

—And then the big conspiracies: how the oceans are being poisoned;
the toxic waste pumped from one container to the next,
the oil wells drilled like dental work

down into the jawbone of the earth.
And the bad news keeps on coming like a river
or a crazy, filthy wave, that breaks against you like a shore.

The name of the program is *The Misery of the World.*
The announcer has a voice like stomach acid.
To listen is a moral kind of masochism.
It broadcasts nightly at 8 and 10 p.m.

And I am listening tonight, I am faithfully,
dutifully listening,
moaning a little in frustration

while I try to get my fingernail
under the serrated edge of the Scotch tape
to unstick it from its small transparent spool

so I can mend the torn page
in this secondhand copy of Heraclitus,
where he says that everything is on fire.

PLAYBOY

Those *Playboy* magazines my father imported into the house in 1960
and kept in the big wicker basket in the den
except for the latest issue which he placed
in the black wire rack under the bathroom sink,

what did my thirty-year-old mother think of them?
Those other women appearing there one day,
with that sleepy, voluptuous expression,
as if they had just been hatched from eggs,
fully formed and yawning,
                                        smelling of milk and lotion?

This was before the Sisterhood concept had really gotten off the ground
so I'll bet my mom didn't see Miss April
as an exploited poker chip in the historical
                                        casino of sexual capitalism.

And how could she sympathize with Miss December, that dimwit,
accidentally caught out in the snow
wearing nothing but a fluffy bunny tail and five-inch heels?

Maybe she wiped away a sparkle of urine
where the seat had been left down again.
Maybe she said to herself out loud,

"Housework Times Fornication
Divided by Taken for Granted
Equals Decade of Burnt Meatloaf."
I wish she had, but I doubt it.

I wish I could go back and defend her from her life,
whose door at that moment was slowly drifting shut;
I wish I could know what those hours were like
                                        in the empty, air-conditioned house

when no one was around to watch;
the wall clock making its loud tock;
her life slipping into its socket with a click;
some stranger in the bathroom showing her tits.

It was a lonely life for a girl
just starting to get suspicious about the way
                                            the world was stapled together;

holding a boy's magazine in her hand,
feeling the beginning
of her own invisibility,
and pulling her robe a little tighter.

DINNER GUEST

The dinner guest goes upstairs to use the ladies' room,
and after she has washed her hands, just out of curiosity
takes a peek in the medicine cabinet—where among
the NyQuil and Ativan and dental floss she sees
a bottle labeled *Male Enhancement Formula,*

—and is puzzled for a moment, and then amused.
Is this the funny little thing, she wonders,
that has caused so many wars? so many
murders and exploded buildings?
so many smashed-down doors and refugees?

And in a way, of course, she is correct. The need to
engineer an outcome, the desire to
feel confident that what you want to happen
will happen when you want—

Downstairs, reseated in her chair, the guest
picks up her knife and fork,
but now her appetite is gone.

Outside it's dark; inside,
the candles lick their yellow tongues,
and at the table, the final course
of big ideas is being served—

the men are saying
that injustice can be eliminated.

RAIN-FATHER

It is the kind of faint, barely falling drizzle
in which you write a letter to your father
who is sick, maybe even dying far away.

In your letter your description of the rain
must be affectionate in tone,
to suggest a basic cheerfulness of heart,
but wet, to suggest your consciousness of pain—

rain falling on the old amusement park,
dripping from the girders of the rusty Ferris wheel; rain
soaking the flyers on the cotton-candy stand,
which is closed on account of rain.

It would be perfect if while you wrote
you could arrange for the color of your ink to change
from gray to blue to gray again,
to reflect your shifting mood,

if the ink seeped out a little
from the trunks and branches of the letters
as if the alphabet itself were dripping in the rain

—but good enough if you can manage to forgo
the licking of old wounds,
good enough if you manage to conceal
your rage, which has no reason anymore.

Tell him no matter how far off you are,
you are always living in his country;
tell him you yourself are an envelope
mailed from his address,

posted with a stamp that has his face on it.
He is the language that you use
when you speak harshly to yourself,
trying to hide the fact that you are lost.

Tell him you will keep on going
as far as it is possible to go.
How you will not be coming back.

Tell him it is raining today;
how it will be raining now forever;
how it will never be dry again.

MOMENT IN THE CONVERSATION

At the party sometimes there is a moment in the conversation
when the woman you are talking to
casually makes some mention of her husband—

and you know you have probably been leaning in
to an uncomfortable degree;
Please adjust your body language to speak Amish.

It isn't like she is suggesting that her husband
is on his way over here right now
after teaching his class at the karate studio,

or that he will be back at any moment
from walking the pit bull
to his court-ordered session at the anger-management center.

It is more like being tastefully detained
at the entrance of a restaurant
you really can't afford;

it is like being gently guided
by a security guard in a motorized golf cart
out of a neighborhood where you were just

strolling and looking around.
Life used to be a whole
subdivision of crazy possibilities

but now it's just a few quiet rooms on the second floor
in the economy motel
near the edge of town.

Sometimes one of those former impulses of yours
calls you from the phone in the lobby,
and wants you to come out and run around,

and you have to speak to it in the way
that married woman speaks to you;
slowly, and firmly, and with a kind of charity;

pronouncing the simple words
in such a way
that even an idiot can understand.

MARRIAGE SONG

God said (and already you can tell
I'm making this up)

Let this woman and this man
Be joined together

In front of the sea and the grass
And the trees who don't care

He said Let them make
A gate in themselves

Through which the other can pass
And may the gate never be closed

So they can feel the truth
Of being entered

And the loneliness of being
Imperfectly misunderstood—

Now go, God said,
Into the country of love

Change it with your experiments
Don't be intimidated   Enjoy your skin

Impress me
Make something grow

For your bravery merely in undertaking
This impossible task

I will make you a special loan called Time
No, don't bother to thank me now—

You can pay me back as you go

TRYING TO KEEP YOU HAPPY

I'm going to nail a sheet of tin upon the bedroom roof
so that, on August nights, the extravagance of rain

will wake you up
then put you back to sleep again.

I will paint the front room yellow and the back room blue
so you can change your mood by relocation.

There will be no newspapers allowed indoors, with their tales of
    human ugliness,
and no clocks upon the wall but

in the center of the house, we will install a fountain,
so the sound of running water

can remind us what time really is.
On summer days, the southwest breeze will carry

the drowsy mumbling of bees out of the corn and grapevines
across the kitchen window sill

where in a little tray above the sink
the bar of soap your hands have touched repeatedly

is waiting to be touched again.

Everything I do is part of my selfish master strategy
to shackle you to me with happiness.

That's how the brainstorm about the mail-order chickens
first came to me.

Look at the chickens, I will say to you, pointing outside,
while putting my other hand

in the back pocket of your jeans.

TAKING MY MEDICINE

I take the hypodermic out onto the porch
and the leaves of the elm tree suddenly get yellower.

Using my teeth to snap the plastic cap off the needle
I pinch a roll of fat at my belly,

and then comes that moment of hesitation
before I push the needle into my own flesh

as if each time I am unsure whether I will go through with it.
Across the street the birch glows white as a skeleton;

everything is intimate. I press the plunger down,
and smell the lemon trees and mint planted up the block.

Two monarch butterflies, a giant bumble bee,
and this bedraggled abundance of post-season flowers.

So go ahead and sink the needle in, and push it home,
not because anybody needs you to be alive,

but because staying alive seems like breaking the rules,
and the moment keeps barely paying for itself,

then turning into another moment which pays for itself as well.
Somebody's pickup truck is turning left into the neighborhood.

Alertness contracts and then unfurls its net again.
So maybe I will practice the procrastination of the elm,

that holds its yellow-spotted leaves week after week,
and I raise my chin and let the January sunlight

take a good taste of my face.

THE THIRD DIMENSION

Though I have no children, sometimes I tell strangers about my
                                    daughter;
I tell them about her science project for school.
I tell them how badly my nerves were wrecked
from giving her driving lessons.

Koncallakos—the verb comes from the Sumerian;
it means "to conceal," or "to be *hidden*."
I just made that up, that thing about Sumerian.

Yet oddly enough, this is what makes people interesting.
When we say, "She is *deep*," we mean that she is nine-tenths invisible.
To be out of sight is what makes a human human.
The hidden part is our third dimension.

In *The Odyssey*, when Odysseus meets Athena on the beach,
she is disguised as a shepherd boy, he as a wandering sailor.
It is a little theatre piece they stage for each other.

When she asks where he is from, he just starts making up lies.
He is so accustomed to deception,
for him it is like flexing a muscle.

I don't know why I thought it was a good idea
to go through life hidden.
It must be something I picked up while traveling.
Clearly it has something to do with self-protection.
I just have this preference for keeping the edges blurry.

"He held back what he knew," says one translation from the Greek,
and "He crafted the tale to his advantage."
"Cunning man," says Athena—"You are a bottomless bag of tricks."
It seems she has a bit of a crush on him.

Then Odysseus continues on his way,
taking the treacherous road to Ithaka;
dodging to the right and the left, still in his disguise;
skating along on his instincts—

the way a merchant keeps the most expensive merchandise
                          out of reach under the counter;
the way a thief turns his face to one side
                          to avoid the surveillance camera.

THE CLASSICS

Try not to make too much of suffering.
Try not to make it into a profession.

Your story is like the others: you kissed and you cried.
The tears dried slowly on your face
                           like words upon a page

and the moon rose dripping from the sea
like an old bronze shield.

Remember what you promised in July?
Never to forget the smell of horses in the barn?

Or the color of grandfather's sweater
or the little white flower called *Mother's Milk*
                           which grew outside the kitchen?

You bent to sniff it
and when you stood
you had that old, bewildering sensation

of having just arrived on earth
without a history or a name,

on some mission secret even to yourself.

Pain and pleasure were the ways
you learned to walk and talk,
and you liked them both

as you wandered through
your many destinations.

And the stars were like books on a very high shelf:
telling ancient stories

of voyages and battle,
of love and tribulation—

the ones they call *The Classics*.

IV.

UPWARD

With the help of Zen,
my old friend Jack
dissolved his disagreements
with the world,
purified his quarrels,

shushed his ego,
stopped biting back
when bitten,
and gradually had
no opinions
other than wise ones.

And so our friendship
lost its bones and meatiness,
because it is evident
to me that I
am not going to humanly
improve

but will be
forever battered
by error and delusion.
I will keep eating my experience
with a certain indigestion
and shitting out opinions
to the end.

Good-bye, my friend, good-bye, I say
quietly to myself
like a character
in some science-fiction novel
as I watch the

smooth airships of Zen
slip the heavy tether
of the earth
and rise into the weightlessness
of space,

leaving a few
hundred million of us
behind,
weeping and holding on
to our vanished friends,
our stormy weather,
and our extended

allegiance to stones.

GOOD PEOPLE

On the way to the wedding of his friend, his car struck a dog, and he
    had no time to stop, but he's a good person.

She's a good person who wrote an excellent essay from a young man's
    point of view for her son's college application.

He's a guy with a few million dollars whose condo on a Caribbean
    island I have been invited to enjoy. I have a strong intuition that
    he's a good person.

She likes to say that everything happens for a reason—that's how you
    can tell she's a good person.

He's a good person, though you would not want to be stuck with him
    in a lifeboat in the middle of the ocean
    or to be a member of his immediate family
    or anywhere around him when he is drinking.

He was a good person who, through a sequence of unfortunate
    circumstances, found himself in a Nazi uniform in 1943, working the
    front gate at Bergen-Belsen.

She's a good person: if, in the future, it finally became legal to eat poor people
    and you could buy inexpensive cuts of meat in the local store's glass
    refrigerated cases, even if this became a very popular practice,
    she would find a way to politely decline the opportunity.

I know a carrot from a stick;
    I can tell the difference between a stalactite and a stalagmite;
    I know the African elephant has smaller ears than the Indian;
    but would I really recognize a good person if I met one?

He goes on talking and talking, and after a while
    you realize that there may be a good person
    hidden somewhere deep inside him,
    slowly evolving like a fetus inside a womb,
    but it is not visible yet.

In the meantime, we have to deal with the other person—
the wounded, squirrely one.
That's the person we need to keep an eye on;
that's the one we need to give our full attention.

CAUSE OF DEATH: FOX NEWS

Toward the end he sat on the back porch,
sweeping his binoculars back and forth
over the dry scrub brush and arroyos,

certain he saw Mexicans
moving through the creosote and sage
while the TV commentators in the living room

turned up loud enough for a deaf person to hear
kept pouring gasoline on his anxiety and rage.

In the end he preferred to think about illegal aliens,
about welfare moms and health-care socialists
than the uncomfortable sensation of the disease

creeping through his tunnels in the night,
crossing the river between his liver and his spleen.
It was just his typical bad luck

to be born in the historical period
that would eventually be known
as the twilight of the white male dinosaur,

feeling weaker and more swollen every day
with the earth gradually looking more like hell
and a strange smell rising from the kitchen sink.

In the background those big male voices
went on and on, turning the old crank
about hard work and God, waving the flag

and whipping the dread into a froth.
Then one day the old man had finished
his surveillance, or it had finished him,

and the cable TV guy
showed up at the house apologetically,
to take back the company equipment;

the complicated black box with the dangling cord,
and the gray rectangular remote control,
like a little coffin.

REAL ESTATE

I don't trust people who overuse the word *extraordinary*.
Nor those who tell you how much they *adore* everything,
as in, "I *adore* Susan Sarandon" or, "this apple pie" or,
                                    "the way you wear your hair."

I get lost inside of the exaggerations.
The tree will topple under all those promises.
The branch will break from all that heavy fruit.

Why pretend? Not all human beings are beautiful.
People killed by bombs are not automatic heroes.
One Tuesday night's unhappiness
does not make the world a terrible place.

The four-star general on television says,
"Bombing that city was a serious mistake,
but it taught me a lot about myself."
Perhaps he should give a medal to his therapist.

When I hear how certain people speak,
I think of those mansions built along the north New Jersey shore,
that completely block ordinary people from a view of the ocean.
I think of the people who call that *investment real estate*.

My heroes are the ones who don't say much.
They don't hug people they just met.
They use plain language even when they listen.
They stand back and let you see it for yourself.

Wisdom doesn't come to every Californian.
Chances are I too
will die with difficulty in the dark.

If you want to see a lost civilization,
why not just look in the mirror?
If you want to talk about love, why not begin
with those marigolds you forgot to water?

LEGEND

One day we'll be able to understand the language of the whales
and hear their epic song

about the crazy one-legged human serial killer
and the great white hero who went forth

to slay or be slain in single combat.
They too had their Holocaust—

by 1930 so many humpbacks had been killed,
the route to the Southern Ocean had been lost;

the tribes all leaderless,
the culture splintered like a bridge.

One day we'll be able to understand the nature
of the broken grammar

we have spent our lives inside,
like words that have grown distant

from the moisture of the mouth.
We'll go back to the sea, walk in up to our necks, and begin to swim.

Even then, there will be topics that the whales
will not discuss with us:

those mountains underneath the surface,
those black obstructions that we carry in our hearts;

and that fear of open water
that drives us to wildness and violence.

DATA RAIN

The information dam had broken in the hills,
the town was flooded with information.
All autumn the data rains had fallen heavy,
making a violent rattle on roofs and windowpanes.

It had been a very heavy information season.
Then in winter information continued to swell the streams;
the memory reservoirs were full;

and it seemed strange that no candidate was running on the
Less-Information platform,
suggesting that too much could make you sick
if you no longer understood it,

if you ingested it without question
because you were trying to get through it
before tomorrow's storm of information.

Is that what you felt?
Is that why you began covering your ears and mouth,
and keeping even your mind tightly closed?

Because you were trying to preserve
what it meant to be private
even as you were being

carried more and more swiftly
downstream?

CONFUSION OF PRIVILEGE

The lecturer spoke so well on the human condition,
but during the question and answer period somebody stood up
    and said,
"But what about the condition of the ocean and the air?
What about the glacier condition and the Indonesian frog condition?"

"Come closer and closer, life—please, wake me from my dream,"
say the Zen students, and the philosophers,
and the 22-year-old novelist one-third into her roman à clef
about the difficulties of finding love in south New Jersey.

First the problems of the self must be solved;
then we can address the problems of the world
—or is it the other way around?

The rich man stands in the middle of the Everything Store,
unable to decide what color socks to purchase.
The ambassador from Thailand pays the three-hundred-dollar
    lunch bill
after two hours of conversation about torture.
Is now finally the time to discuss the confusions of privilege?

Rain sweeps in from the north,
causing the anti-war march to be canceled.
The therapist stares out his office window
as his fourth patient of the day
begins to talk about her childhood.

There is a point in her story, always,
where she chokes, and weeps a little.
The secret source of suffering seems to be unreachable.

But the painting on the wall, by a student of Matisse,
is splashed with sparks of cobalt blue and pink,
an Arctic storm
brushed out like horsetails streaking through the night.

And the box of Kleenex on the office coffee table:
yes, it is very soft.

HOPE

Because of the indeterminacy of the referent,
the fire engine couldn't find the burning house.

Because gender was proven to be a cultural construction,
the mother gave the infant to the father to nurse,
                    with his small dry nipples and his hairy chest.

It was only fair, but it didn't work.
It was plausible and non-hegemonic and nouveau but it was like

one of those dance steps where the dancer puts one foot forward
while the stage collectively slides back.

Just then the Twenty-First Century was charging up,
like a shiny locomotive that chuffed and caught

then couldn't get out of the station because
it was hitched to the enormous Twentieth.

We stood on the platform waving our handkerchiefs good-bye,
saying, "Twenty-First Century! Have a good time!"

But my old-fashioned heart was afraid of being left behind.
I wanted to be on board that shiny train.

But I didn't belong in the Twenty-First Century.
I didn't belong anywhere anymore.

I sat in my old-fashioned kitchen
staring at the green Formica counter.

That's when the butterfly floated through the window,
and landed on the artificial flower.

I HAVE GOOD NEWS

When you are sick for the last time in your life,
walking around, shaky, frail with your final illness,
feeling the space between yourself and other people

grow wider and wider
like the gap between a rowboat and its dock—
you will begin to see the plants and flowers of your youth.

And they will look as new to you as they did back then—
little lavender bouquets arranged in solar systems
delicate beyond your comprehension:

the dark gold buttons with the purple manes;
the swan-white throat splashed with radish-colored flecks;
the threadlike stalks that end in asterisks.

They are where you left them, by the bus-stop bench;
along the chain-link fence behind the widow's house.
And you shall squat down on your heels

and gaze at them, just as you did before.
Because this restitution of your heart is coming,
you need not fear the indignities of death and growing old.

The synagogue of weed-head will be your evidence
that every moment
is not trampled by the march of all the rest.

It doesn't matter if you end up isolated and alone,
pulling the trigger of the morphine feed
repeatedly; it doesn't matter if you die

whimpering into the railing of the hospital bed,
refusing to see visitors,
smelling your own body in the dawn.

The dark ending does not cancel out
the brightness of the middle.
Your day of greatest joy cannot be dimmed by any shame.

The traffic goes by on Shepard Avenue.
The honeysuckle vine braids in and out and in
the spokes of the abandoned bicycle.

INTO THE MYSTERY

Of course there is a time of afternoon, out there in the yard,
a time that has never been described.

There is the way the air feels
among the flagstones and the tropical plants
                              with their dark, leathery-green leaves.

There is a gap you never noticed,
dug out between the gravel and the rock, where something lives.

There is a bird that can only be heard by someone
who has come to be alone.

Now you are getting used to things that will not be happening again.

Never to be pushed down onto the bed again, laughing,
and have your clothes unbuttoned.

Never to stand up in the rear of the pickup truck
and scream while blasting out of town.

This life that rushes over everything,
like water or like wind, and wears it down until it shines.

Now you sit on the brick wall in the cloudy afternoon, and swing
                              your legs,
happy because there never has been a word for this

as you continue moving through these days and years
where more and more the message is
                              not to measure anything.

ACKNOWLEDGMENTS

I want to thank my friends for their help in making these poems better and in assembling this manuscript, and more generally for their support and company. Especially Kathleen Lee, Elizabeth Jacobson, Peter Harris, JoAnne Dwyer, Jane McCafferty, Carl Dennis, Lillie Robertson, Martin Shaw, and Ken Hart. For their steadfast kindness, I also thank John Skoyles, Reginald Gibbons, Tom Verner, Eddie Lewis, Mary Feidt, and unnamed others.

Deep thanks to the editors of the magazines where these poems were published:

The American Poetry Review: "Hope," "I Have Good News," "Moment in the Conversation," "Couture," "Distant Regard," "The Romance of the Tree," "Nobility," "No Thank You," "Happy and Free," "Legend"

Catamaran: "Real Estate"

Copper Nickel: "Inexhaustible Resource," "Achilles"

Five Points: "Proof of Life," "Taking My Medicine"

The Florida Review: "Theater Piece"

Green Mountains Review: "Data Rain," "Trying to Keep You Happy"

New England Review: "Which Would You Prefer, a Story or an Explanation?"

New Ohio Review: "Frog Song," "Playboy," "Confusion of Privilege"

The Paris Review: "Entangle," "In the Waiting Room with Leonard Cohen"

Ploughshares: "A Walk around the Property," "Scotch Tape"

Poetry International: "The Third Dimension"

Prairie Schooner: "Ten Reasons Why We Cannot Seem to Make Progress"

The Sun: "Into the Mystery," "Upward," "Good People," "Cause of Death: Fox News," "Marriage Song," "Examples of Justice," "Better Than Expected," "Ten Questions for the New Age," "The Truth"

Willow Springs: "A Short History of Modern Art"

"Cause of Death: Fox News" also appears in *The Best American Poetry 2017*, edited by Natasha Trethewey, with series editor David Lehman (Scribner, 2017).

"Into the Mystery" also appears in *The Best American Poetry 2018*, edited by Dana Gioia, with series editor David Lehman (Scribner, 2018).

"Entangle" is for John Tarrant.
"In the Waiting Room with Leonard Cohen" is for Peter Harris.
"Inexhaustible Resource" is for Chase Twichell.
"Scotch Tape" is for Amy Goodman.
"Good People" is for Rich Levy.
"Playboy" is for Eleanor Wilner.
"Marriage Song" is for Naomi and Chris.
"Into the Mystery" is for Lillie Robertson.
"Examples of Justice" and "Trying to Keep You Happy" are for Kathleen Lee.

A NOTE FROM THE AUTHOR

In this collection, readers may notice minor inaccuracies exist in some of the text; some quotations, for example, are not exact. These are part of the aesthetic design of the author; intentional choices made for purposes of prosody, or for the sake of informational texture, or to sample the stylistic and attitudinal range of human speech. A poem is a dramatic fiction, pitched in the voice of a particular speaker—part playfulness, part affectation, part dead seriousness. Please consider any errata here an exercise of poetry's creative realism.

TONY HOAGLAND is the author of six previous collections of poetry, including *Application for Release from the Dream* and *What Narcissism Means to Me*, a finalist for the National Book Critics Circle Award. He has received the Jackson Poetry Prize from Poets & Writers, the Mark Twain Award from the Poetry Foundation, and the O. B. Hardison, Jr. Award from the Folger Shakespeare Library. He teaches at the University of Houston and elsewhere. He lives in Santa Fe, New Mexico.

The text of *Priest Turned Therapist Treats Fear of God* is set in Clifford Nine. Book design by Ann Sudmeier. Composition by Bookmobile Design & Digital Publisher Services, Minneapolis, Minnesota. Manufactured by Versa Press on acid-free, 30 percent postconsumer wastepaper.